Morality Shorts

Short, Short Stories with a
Moral Poetic Twist

Miatta Lynn Lansana

authorHOUSE®

AuthorHouse™
1663 Liberty Drive
Bloomington, IN 47403
www.authorhouse.com
Phone: 1-800-839-8640

Published by AuthorHouse 2/22/2012

ISBN: 978-1-4685-0792-8 (e)
ISBN: 978-1-4685-0793-5 (hc)
ISBN: 978-1-4685-0794-2 (sc)

Library of Congress Control Number: 2011962053

Little Johnny Maple's Prayer

While sitting in a church on a cold winter day little Johnny Maple began to pray "dear heavenly Father, please show me your son's face; if you show me his face all my pain will go away." While little Johnny Maple prayed a light from God began to shine on his face; all who stood by began to tremble with fear saying, "what manner of child is this? He has brought the presence of God here." No one touched little Johnny Maple as he trembled on the church's ground with a band of angels all around. Members of the church denied this remarkable act, and stared at

Johnny as if they did not want him to come back. The angels disappeared, and Johnny stood upon his legs strengthen within his heart he was spiritually aware, but they would not believe even though they see him standing up out of his wheelchair. Seeing the hardness of their hearts he began to cry out, "why are you questioning this miracle that came straight from God's heart? God's healing powers still exist today, and our faith is what makes it happen in our lives each and every day." The elder Christians didn't say a word they just closed their eyes and covered their ears to what they just seen and heard. Little Johnny Maple hurt by the hardness of their hearts; pushed his wheelchair to the door saying, "I pray God will reveal himself to this church in a mighty way; because it is not right for Christians to play with their faith." He then pushed his wheelchair right out the door. Never to be seen or heard of by them anymore.

The End

Hidden Treasures

There was an old lady who had a few stories she loved to tell to her seven grandsons Matt, Mark, Luke, John, Paul, Peter, and Wendell. She would tell them stories about her childhood, and how God brought her through. She would tell them all the places she's been, and all she had gone through. All these stories her seven grandsons understood, but the last one she told they didn't see any earthly good. It was the one that one day would save their lives; it was the one about God's son Jesus the Christ. As they sat there, she would talk about this man who came to

Earth and die for their sins; and he didn't stop there, he rose from the grave to sit at the right hand of his Father until this very day. They didn't understand until their grandmother died, and they were searching for the true meaning of life.

Matt, Mark, Luke, John, Paul, Peter, and Wendell searched through the stories she'd tell. After searching and searching they remembered a part that was in all the stories their grandmother use to share that was so unique. It was the part about the Holy Bible that helped her in good times and in tragedy. They searched high and low in their grandmother's room for that hidden treasure. The Holy Bible, the seven knew they needed; after searching for hours Wendell the seventh grandson spotted a brown box with some kind of writing on it. "What does it say?" He wasn't able to tell. He just called the others over as he broke off the seal. When it was open they all looked with surprise because there it was The Holy Bible, and a picture of them and their grandmother standing with Jesus hidden inside.

The End

The Golden Key

There was a little girl named Annie-Bell who had a sure plan of not going to Hell. She kept the plan in a box that had a golden key in which kept it locked. Many asked Annie-Bell what was her plan, but she knew If they didn't know God they wouldn't understand; so Annie-Bell kept her plan within her soul, so much so She didn't let anyone know. Annie-Bell grew old, but her heart remained the same; she still possessed the plan in a box with a golden key in which kept it locked. Many others asked Annie-Bell what was her plan, but she knew if they didn't know God they wouldn't understand. Therefore, Annie-Bell died not telling a soul of the plan they wanted and needed to know. Annie-Bell was buried with the box that had a golden key in which kept it locked. She ascended up to Heaven, and stood at the pearly gates waiting to her savior's face. When Jesus came he had a frown, and Annie-Bell's head began to hang down. "Why didn't you share what was in the box that had a golden key in which kept it locked?" Asked Jesus. "They didn't know you and I didn't think they would understand." Answered Annie-Bell. "Didn't you know that was a part of the plan; to seek and to save that which is lost that was the whole message of my cross." Therefore, Annie-Bell enter Heaven not receiving her full reward because she wouldn't do what God had sent her here for.

The End

The Virgin

There once was virgin that sat by the road waiting for a prince to come by, and as she sat by the road a young man on a bike stopped to say "hi". He was not exactly what she was looking for, but she got tired of waiting so she took a stroll with him to the shore. After spending a few hours with him she knew he wasn't right, so she ended the conversation by saying "it was nice meeting you, have a happy life." She got up and left the shore, and return to the side of the road to wait some more, but as she sat down in her common place she notice sand all over the place. It was on her shoes, stockings, and dress. She began to feel insecure about not looking her best. As she began to sigh a man in a car stopped by to say "hi." He wasn't exactly what she was looking for, but she decided to go for a spend once more.

They took a spend to the park just before it was getting dark. They sat there and talked for hours, but she just wasn't his flower, so he got up and said "good-bye," while she sat there and cried. As she was crying it began to rain, but she couldn't move because of her pain and shame. A man saw her crying and ran to her aide, but she was so heartbroken she didn't even see his princely face. He carried her to his chariot, and commanded the driver to go. He held her in his arms and comforted her wounded soul, but the poor virgin still didn't know. It wasn't until he called out her new name "Princess," that she realized things had finally changed.

The End

The Iron

There once was an iron that decided it didn't want to be an iron anymore, so it went out to explore its possibilities. It came up to a little girl trying to comb her hair, but she had no mirror anywhere. The iron immediately thought to its self "this is a job I can do, I will just turn to my silver side, and she will be able to see herself," but the little girl laughed and the iron began to sigh. "You're just an iron, and I can't see my reflection on your silver side," laughed the little girl. The iron went away sad not knowing its place when all of a sudden it seen a woman with an angry look on her face. The woman's toaster had broken, and she didn't see how she was going to make her husband toast before he went over- seas. The iron immediately thought to its self "this is a job I can do, I'll just plug myself up, and she can lay me flat, I know I can do that," but the woman laughed and the iron began to sigh. "You're just an iron you can't toast bread on both sides at the same time," laughed the woman. The iron went away sad not knowing its place when all of a sudden it seen a boy freezing cold all over the place. The iron immediately thought to its self this is a job I can do, I will just plug myself up, and the heat will come streaming through, but the boy laughed and the iron began to sigh. "You're just an iron you can't heat up a room of this size," laughed the boy. Once again the iron went away sad not knowing its place when all of a sudden it seen a man with a hopeless look on his face. The man lost his iron, and he had to be at a job interview that he scheduled last week. The iron immediately thought to its self I know this is a job that I can do because this is what I was created to do.

The man when he saw the iron was glad, and thanked God with every breath he had.

The End

The Unforgivable Death

There once was a man who got so offended he's heart became as stone. Everywhere that this man went he commanded everyone to leave him alone. On many occasions he would go to the corner market to get some groceries. While in the market he would always see someone who offended him or his family, and when he saw them he would avoid them with all his might, not even wanting them to be in his sight. He avoided the aisles he knew they would be in, and he even neglected to get some of his groceries, but one unforgettable day things would change in a deadly way. He'd arrived at the corner market on a very hot day, and headed to the frozen food section to get some cool air, but just as he was about to walk down the aisle he saw one of the unforgivable standing there. He couldn't believe his eyes; his chest began to swell, as his heart became hot as Hell. He turned from that aisle and proceeded toward the cold drinks to try to relieve himself from all the heat, but to his surprise when he arrived there he could see another unforgivable standing there drinking a cold soft drink. He was so angry and began to go into a rage when he thought to himself "a bag of ice would help me out on such a hot day." He proceeded toward the ice when he noticed less than thirty feet another unforgivable standing in front of the ice chest trying to relieve himself from the heat. He couldn't take it anymore, he was outraged, he just fell on the floor in the corner market and died, while many of the unforgivable gathered around asking "how, when, and why?"

The End

One-Eighty

There once was a boy who liked to live a dangerous life style. Any opportunity offered to him to do wrong that he would do going the extra mile. He was proud, and often bragged about the evil he's done, who'd ever guess that he was a preacher's son. He would hang on street corners drinking brew with his friends, and before the day was over he'd rob old ladies and old men. His earthly father was fed up with his behavior and his heavenly father too, so his heavenly father told his earthly father to pray and he'd see him through. The earthly father took the heavenly father's advice, and prayed for his son every day and every night, but the change he'd hoped for he could barely see. His son began to turn into a zombie. His son wouldn't talk to him and it seemed like he didn't sleep, he was pale, and wouldn't eat. The earthly father was sad, and wondered if he was doing the right thing by trusting God and not doing anything. The heavenly father read the earthly father's mind, and began to remind him of how he brought him through tough times. The earthly father was comforted by his heavenly father's words, and began reminiscing about the days when he too was lacking self-worth. The earthly father began to cry, realizing now for the very first time how God really changed his life, and if he could change a liar, drug addict, and a very violent man. How much more will he do for the son of that man?

The End

I Hate Black

There once was a young white boy who hated every race especially blacks, and every time he went to town he would see black people and negatively react. He would yell out "go home nigger!" as loud as he could, and say to the white person next to him "those niggers are no earthly good." While in town he would tell the most hateful jokes, jokes like "if you ever see a nigger on my side of town you know the rope broke." His humor impressed many especially the Klan; they would always tell him "if you keep this up we will have no choice but to make you our right hand man." The Klan's words had a very strong effect, and the young white boy wanted to prove he was legit, so he got a rope and found a little black child, and asked him if he'd like to go bike riding for a while. The little black child said "yes," with his angelic smile, while the young white boy put him on his bike, and rode about a half of a mile. The young white boy stopped in front of an old Oak tree, and they got off the bike. He then got the rope, and suggested they make a swing. He told the little black child to tie the rope around his shoulders, so he could test out everything. The little black child did as he was told to do, and tied the rope around his shoulders as tight as he knew. The young white boy tied the other end of the rope to a tire that was sitting at the end of the tree. He then sat in it, and watched the little black child being lifted off his feet. Screaming, and screaming, gasping for air the little black child stopped, and hung there. The young white boy got up, and the little black child fell down. All at once it hit the young white boy that everything in his life would be black now.

The End

The Judgmental Woman

There once was a woman who loved very rich and handsome men, and if a man were not rich and handsome she wouldn't give him a chance. Men would often call her a "gold digging witch," but that didn't seem to bother her especially if they weren't handsome and rich. One night while she was in a club a very common looking, blue collared man came up to ask her if she would like to dance. She replied back "by the look of your shoes you're not rich enough for me, and by the look of your face you're not good looking to me." The man was hurt, most of all surprised, how could she say such evil words without even blinking her eyes. The man being very angry wanted to get revenge, so he waited to the party was over and attacked her in the presence of her friends.

He beat her so bad she could hardly see, and then he ran off before he was caught by the police. She laid there in a pool of blood; it was such an ugly sight to see. She spent three months in the hospital isolated from her family and friends. When the three months had ended the doctors removed the bandages from her face, and the beauty that she was use to had vanished without a trace. She was devastated, and she then began to cry, "Who is gone to love me, now that the only good thing about me is gone out of my life?" The woman was soon released from the hospital, and felt in her heart no other choice but to isolate herself. "Who'd ever thought this would happen to such a beautiful woman, just by her negatively judging someone else."

The End

Scary Mary

There once was an old lady name Mary, who everyone thought was a little scary. They would make up horrible rumors about her old house, and tell ugly rumors about her, especially one in which they say she ate a mouse. Almost everyone in the neighborhood could agree that old lady Mary was a little scary. What made her scary they couldn't tell, maybe it was her eyes that had the appearance of hell, or maybe it was that time she went to jail. For whatever reason there was no one who could trust her especially around his or her kids. One spring day old lady

Mary went out in her garden to pass some time away when all of a sudden she looked up and seen a neighborhood boy known by the name of Gary. "Hi, old lady Mary," he softly said as he reached out and touched her leg.

Old lady Mary was very surprised, so much so she started to cry. Gary asked her why she was crying so, and old lady Mary replied back "I don't know." "Maybe I'm crying because no one cared to see how their ugly rumors were taking a negative effect on me." Gary began to cry and feel pain as well realizing her eyes were too beautiful to have the appearance of hell, and then he began to see how she must have felt being alienated by everyone else.

The End

Only Words

There once was a man who didn't care about what he would say, and every time someone would try to correct him hatred would fill his face. "Don't you try to correct me!" He would shout, so much so people would space him out. The man's mean words seemed to have no effect until he met up with a boy named Jet. Jet was a loner, and didn't do well in school, and he was an outcast because people were so rude. One day Jet decided to ditch school, and hang out at the park on a sunny afternoon. The man decided to go to the park as well before he took advantage of the blue light sale. Jet got to the park a little before the man did, and decided to rest under the only Oak tree. The man was about a block away when he began to think of that old Oak tree shade, but when he got to the park he was surprised to see that a young boy was already sitting there.

"What are you doing here?" The man asked. Jet looked up and started to laugh. "What so funny, are you stupid or something?" The man replied. Jet just sat there quietly and began to sigh. "Did you hear me you stupid son of a gun? Why don't you get out of my spot, and stop acting like a bum. Jet's feelings were hurt and he began to cry, while the man waved in his face and told him "good-bye." Jet got up and began to walk away when he notices a bridge and under it high water was laid. Jet walked over to the bridge, and thought about jumping off when a voice said inside him "don't do it, it's not worth the cost," but behind him he could hear the man shouting "why don't you jump, and put your mother out of her shame." The man turned away and laughed, but Jet didn't, he drowned that day while the man cried, "they were only words, I didn't mean to hurt the little guy."

The End

Great, but Worthless

There once was a woman who really loved life, and everything she did she made sure to do it at least twice. She faced every challenge and dared not to quit. She was graceful and beautiful, and stood about five feet nine. There was no doubt about it men thought she was fine, so fine; men didn't have any problems asking her on a date. Heck, with her looks and their money it was fate. She was popular with women too, and everything she would ware and do they would ware and do the same things too. No one had a bad word to say about her, to them she is the greatest woman who ever walked the earth, but what they didn't know is that this great woman neglected her soul.

She had everything in the world going for her, but in heaven she would not be because she did not believe. Many tried to tell her about Jesus, but she would respond back "believing in Jesus is a big mistake." When they asked her "why" she responded "I'm beautiful, popular, powerful, and successful. What would a woman like me need a God for? God is for poor hopeless people to adore." They who asked went away grieved, and wonder in their hearts "how could someone who has achieve so many of her goals be totally worthless in her soul?"

The End

Nobodies Friend

There once was a boy who didn't like himself, and he couldn't have good relationships with anyone else. He tried and tried to make friends, but before he knew it he had one more enemy, and one less friend. He didn't understand why his fortune was so bad, and why every friend made him feel so sad. After his relationships would end he would mope around for days wondering why the relationship had to end in such a negative way. Once the boy became a man he was presented another chance to be a friend. He was a great friend in the very start, but his hatred for himself began to place its ugly mark. His new friend would ask him "man, why are you so hard on yourself?" His new friend would also advise him "if you don't respect yourself, you won't get any respect from anyone else." The man would look in space as these words were being spoken; not realizing his attitude about himself was the reason why his relationships were choking. Once again he lost his friend, but this time he was determined not to let the friendship end. He had been broken hearted to many times before, and he wasn't going to allow it to happen anymore. He began to plot a way to kill his ex-friend, so finally he could be the one who brought something to an end. He waited outside his ex-friend's job, and created a scene, so much so there was a mob. His ex-friend headed out to see what was going on, but by the time he made it out there the mob was gone. He was headed back in when suddenly he heard a gun cock. He turned around, and saw the man with his jaws locked. "What are you doing man?" The ex-friend cried. The man was silent, consumed in his own personal thoughts, when suddenly the plot he had got lost. An angel came down and knocked the man's gun to the ground. The angel grabbed the man's face and looked him in the eyes, and said "don't hurt someone else because you feel so much hatred for yourself, and that's why you have so hard of a time keeping friends because of the hatred within."

The End

What Goes Around

There once was a girl who didn't care about what she would do, and she didn't even think twice about the pain she was putting others through. She would stay out very late at night, and she would let strange men hold her tight. She would ditch school, do drugs, drink alcohol to be cool, and among the company of her friends she always acts like a fool. Her mother was so grieved to see her act so, but she knew she had no other choice but to pray, and let her go. The girl being pushed into womanhood because of the birth of her child, grew up mentally, and stopped acting wild. She became a successful young woman, with a beautiful child. She thought all her bad days were behind her now, so she began to relax in the good life, and married one of the men who use to hold her tight.

Everything seemed great, everything seemed fine until her daughter got a little older, and started losing her mind. She did everything her mother did, but took it a little further. Her mother was devastated, and began to curse her. The mother could not understand where her sweet little girl could have gotten her evil ways, until she took a long look in an old mirror one day.

The End

Bitter to the Core

There once was a man who'd always pray for tomorrow to come, and no matter what kind of day he was having he would hope for the next one. He wasn't content with the life he lived, and many would ask him "why don't you change?" But he would respond with a laugh "tomorrow won't be the same." Once again he woke up into a day in which he was not satisfied; his wife couldn't understand why he felt so void inside. He had many thoughts about leaving his job, city, and home, but couldn't do it feeling that it would be wrong. He began to withdraw being very bitter, so much so being near his wife made his body quiver. His wife couldn't understand why he avoided her so, and why he didn't seem to love her anymore. She turned to the comfort of a close family friend; he comforted her so much a relationship started.

The man had no ideal his friend was involved with his wife, and to be honest at the time he wouldn't even care as long as he didn't have to hold her tight. The man decided to take a vacation to get away from things, and while he was alone he begun to appreciate his wife, and ware his wedding ring. He came back home three weeks later expecting to see his loving wife's face, but instead came back to an empty house, and a letter that read "I'm leaving you!

Sincerely,

Grace."

The End

Just Like Dad

There once was a boy who was very sad, and always promised not to be like his dad. He hated everything his dad would do, and he hated him even more for what he put his mother through. His dad would come in drunk, and beat his mother until she bled, leaving big knots all over her head. The boy would watch helplessly and cry, while rage and anger built up inside. He saw this violence all his life, until he moved out and got himself a wife. At first his marriage seemed perfect, not a problem in sight. Then situations happened that would change his life; his wife got pregnant, he lost his job, and all his wife wanted to do was argue and call him a fat slob. The rage and anger begin to arise in his heart, so he began to stay out late, so he wouldn't fall apart.

He began to drink alcohol more than he used to, and he was becoming more and more detached from the world he knew. His wife began to notice it and argue with him even more, until one day he couldn't take it anymore. He grabbed her head and slammed it to the kitchen floor. She cried and screamed while he banged her head once more, and there she laid unconscious on the floor. When he saw her laying there his head began to ring, while a voice yelled inside his head "you're just like me son, I knew you would do such a thing!"

The End

Faking

There once was a woman who couldn't be real, and she wouldn't tell people how she really felt. She would smile in people's faces that she felt did her so much wrong, so much so they didn't even know she knew what was going on. She would cry behind closed doors, and then come out with a smile. Those who mistreated her, were always amazed at for them she would go that extra mile, but inside she was becoming cold as ice because of them not treating her right. One day she got a call from one of those friends who stabbed her in the back by taking her man. "Hey girl, long time no see, why don't you come over here and hang out with me?" She was angry at her request, but she choked it all in and said "I will be over there in ten minutes Jess." She hung up the phone, and began to sigh "how could I even talk to her when she didn't even apologize."

Her anger became outrage, and all she could think about was seeing that witches face. She arrived at her house exactly ten minutes later, while parking her car she pictured feeding her ex-friend to the alligators. She got out of her car, and walked up to the door. Her ex-friend saw her and ran to welcome her in; little did she know home-girl was there for revenge. With her famous fake smile on her face she walked into her ex-friend's place, and took a seat on the comfortable couch, and then started running her mouth. She talked about almost everything, so much so her ex-friend wished the fat lady would sing, but there was no fat lady in the room so she turned on their favorite tune. Listening to the music brought back memories, and the woman remembered how much she was deceived by her ex-friend who took her man, so she knew at that moment she had to stick with her plan. She asked her ex-friend for a drink, while she was in the kitchen the woman grabbed a hammer thinking within herself "man, I can't stand her." Her ex-friend came back with her drink, and the woman hid the hammer under the seat waiting for the right time. Feeling good about her plan she began to drink the drink prepared by her ex-friend. After drinking the drink the woman fell to the floor never to be seen alive anymore.

The End

One-Sided Love

There once was a woman who loved a man, so much so no one around her could understand. He was not the best man on the earth she could pick, but to her he was the best she could get. She never could understand why others thought he was so wrong, and why they always encouraged her to move on. This was something that plagued her every day of her life, until one unfortunate night. It was a night they promised to spend together; it was a night her life on earth would end forever. It was a night he showed up on time, and it was a night he cross the line. It didn't matter

how much she told him "no," he just wouldn't let her go.
She cried out to him "I thought you loved me," but in love
with her he didn't want to be. To him she was nothing, but
a piece of meat, and to him she was the town's freak.

For him all the respect he had for her was gone
before they even began to date. For him it was nothing to
rape her, and drown her in the lake. For her it was painful
fore she gave her heart to this man, and for her his brutality
toward her she didn't understand.

She screamed and cried with her face in the water,
and his hands tightly around the back of her neck, and she
wonder why "he didn't really love her?" As she pasted from
life to death.

The End

Fear

There once was a man who had fear, and everything he would do the fear would appear. He was locked in a prison of his mind, and hinder in his life all the time. He tried desperately to overcome his fears, but soon as he overcame one another would appear. As the years went by he became weary and stop trying, and he often had thoughts of dying. Committing himself to life on death row he knew he'd lost all control. Lying in a bed of total despair, he began to question "why God put him here?" A question that God seemed to ignore, which made him wallow in that bed of despair even more. He had no one around him to help him see the light, so the darkness filled up inside of him causing even more fright. Lying in that bed of despair he decided he didn't want to live anymore, so he grabbed his 45 next to his Bible out of his drawer. Holding the gun in his hand he couldn't believe that he was going to be the one to bring his life to an end. Placing the gun to his head and lying back on his bed, that bed of despair is where he cried, and that bed of despair is where he would die, but not because he didn't have a choice, he just feared listening to God's voice. The voice that said, "Fore God didn't give us a spirit of fear," and the voice that said, "Be careful of what you hear." It was all spoken in the Bible of course, but still it was God's voice.

The End

Power of the Tongue

There once was girl from age one to twenty-two who always would say what she would be and do. She became all she said, and she did all she said she would do, but after age twenty-two all her goals were accomplished and through. She didn't realize it was time for her to make others, but instead of making new goals she sat around and said words that no human should utter. It wasn't long before her words began to take effect, and make her life not at its best. She couldn't understand why things were going so wrong, and she couldn't understand why she didn't want to live on. Every time she went through this depression her words would go into even more negative aggression. Sitting in a whirlwind of her negative words, her negative words are all she heard. "You're never going to be anything, you're best days were in your past, and if something did work out for you, you know it wouldn't last." All these negative words ran through her mind and out her mouth day and night, so much so she began to pick up a crack pipe. Smoking and smoking, smoking her life away, but she didn't realize it wasn't her smoking it was her words really take her life away. Sitting in her room smoking on a crack pipe in total despair she began to wonder if God really cared, and God reading her thoughts and feeling her despair gave her a vision of her former life to show her how much he does care. He showed her in the vision how positive her words use to be and how everything she thought and said he made sure she'd seen. The woman thought to herself how the vision was so true how everything she said from age one to twenty- two she had gone through. Then the woman thought to herself about the negative words she's been saying lately, and that how they have affected her life greatly.

The End

A Fool's Reward

There once was a girl who was a fool, and no one around her could control the things she would do. She thought she was cunning, and she thought she was wise, but the only thing she didn't think was a bigger fool was growing inside. The more she thought the worst she got; a fool on a mission was her only plot. She woke up each morning with nothing but foolishness on her mind, but one morning she woke up and would think that way for the last time. It was a morning the sun was shining bright, and it was a morning her foolishness would change her whole life. It was a morning her heart was filled with needs, and it was the morning she would reap every foolish seed. On that morning she got out of bed with nothing but foolish thoughts running through her head. She thought in her mind she would not go to school and then she could hang around the mall all day "that would be cool," she thought. She arrived at the mall about a quarter till nine, "ya, I am being a fool, but I sure do look fine," she thought. In all her thinking on this day she never thought this day would end in such a negative way, but indeed it did end tragically all because she acted so foolishly. She should've had her behind in school, but instead her behind became an eye pleasing sight to some dude. A dude that was much older and more foolish than her, and now she was about to find out how much her foolishness was worth. He approached her as only a fool would, and told her "baby girl damn, you're looking good!" She began to be caught up in his foolish essence, not even thinking about "why does this older man want to be in her presence?" The more he talked the more whipped she got, so much so he was able to lead her to his car in the parking lot. When he got her in the car the crazy fool in him she would see as he force her on her back, and pulled his pants to his knees. She cried and screamed, she sounded like a little child, and no one paid any attention to her crying thinking the child must be with its mother because all other children are in school now.

The End

The Pastor

There once was a pastor who had lust in his heart, and every time he found an object to lust for everything around him fell apart. He often would wonder "why his church would not grow?" It never occurred to him it might be because of the defect in his soul. He never tried to deal or get rid of his lust, and whenever someone would confront him about it, he'd easy over with his favorite lines "we're saved by grace and in God I will trust." The more he ignored his lust problem before God the worst he got, so much so he was looking at women in the church parking lot. He would wait until most of the congregation was gone, and then he would walk up to that new convert when she was standing all alone. He would start the conversation off with something religious and sweet, and before the conversation was over he had made plans to meet her at her house the next week. The new convert would walk away wonder why her pastor would approach her in that way. The day came when the pastor and the new convert were to meet, but her door she didn't answer because she didn't want people to think she was a freak. He looked for her the following weekend, but her membership to that church she decided to bring to an end. The new convert went on to another church, and grew closer to the Lord while that old lustful pastor kept cheating on the one he once adored.

The End

Faithless

There once was a woman who didn't have any faith, and every time something greater than her vision could see came to her to do, she would never move her feet out of their place. She hindered many great opportunities that came into her life, all because she wouldn't let faith reign in her mind. She didn't realize how much not having faith was costing her, and she didn't realize how not stepping out on faith would someday bother her. She didn't realize until one summer day when she stepped outside and it began to rain. The rain was so heavy she could hardly see as she drove off in her car to meet some friends and their families. When she had arrived at the location they were supposed to meet she notice there was an old wooden bridge she would have to cross before their faces she could see, but she couldn't visualize herself crossing that bridge in so much rain. Her heart began to fill up with shame as her friends and their families danced in the rain. She thought "if I just put my foot forward, and try it," but her faithless heart wasn't buying it. She stood there for almost thirty minutes in a God ordain shower, while she watched her friends and their families enjoy lives best. She continued to stand on the other side of the bridge, and settle for less. Her friends and their families didn't notice she was on the other side, and she realizing that began to breakdown and cry. Her tears that day mixed with the rain, as she went back home feeling so much shame.

The End

Just a Man

There once was a man who thought he had the world in the palm of his hand. Everything in his environment he seemed to control, and that power he vowed never to let go. He was a mean and hateful man, and the only thing that mattered to him was his own personal plans. He owned a big corporation that made big bank continually, but his family at home he'd hardly ever see. His wife often complained and his children began to act wild, but he was on top of the world he didn't want to stop and be a family man right now. The years went on and the man, his wife, and his children grew older. His wife past, his children moved far away, and the man was left with a heavy weight on his shoulders. He would often think "why didn't I stop and be there for my family, now they're gone, and there's no one here to love me." By the time he began to question the choices in his life he had retired, and began to live an isolated life. None of his children ever thought about coming around to see how he was doing because they too became self-centered, focusing on their careers and neglecting their families. The man begun to live in the past while his life began to fade away fast. The man would visualize his wife still lying beside him in their bed, while he still heard his four children running and playing in his head. He neglected everything that should matter to a man his age, and chose to watch his soul drift away. Life didn't matter to him now, now that his family was gone away, and all the man made money and power in the world couldn't make them stay.

The End

The Ditch

There once was a little girl who began to dig a ditch, and everyone who was ignorant of that ditch became a victim of her ugly trick. She would watch people to see which ones she could trick by leading them to the ditch. The ditch wasn't a big hole in the ground, but it was a place where she controlled everything around. Whatever she wanted when she brought people to the ditch she got it, and no one ever question her about bring them to the ditch because they thought she wouldn't like it. The girl became prosperous because of her ditch-digging plan, but something was about to happen to her that would fill that ditch up with sand. It was a warm spring day, and she had decided to go out and play. She picked a place along-side the road, and she sat down and played with her favorite doll Marigold, when along came a little girl about the age of ten who also practice the ditch digging plan. "Hey there, can I sit down and play with you for a while," said the ten year old girl with a smile. "Sure you can," answered the girl as she play with Marigold's curls. "Wow, that's a pretty doll you got there, I really like her smile, can I play with her for just a little while?" Asked the ten-year-old girl. A little while turned into hours as the sun began to go down, and the little girl knew her mother was expecting her home for dinner now. "It's time for Marigold and I to go," said the little girl as she grabbed for the doll, but the ten year old girl snatched Marigold away, and with her she would stay. The little girl's heart began to be grieved as she thought about how she was deceived, and she did cry all the way home because there was someone else who didn't want to leave the ditch digging plan alone.

The End

I'm a Man

There once was a man who entered a town where he was the only one with a painted face. The other people in the town would look at him as if he was some kind of disgrace. He was a talented man, and many great things he was able to do, but the townspeople would not give him a chance because his skin resembled the color blue. The man wanted so much in this town to build his life, but because of the color of his skin the people of the town wouldn't treat him right. The man went from middle class living to poverty all because the people in the town wouldn't let him be free. The man would not leave the town in order to better his life because he knew that same spirit that was in that town would follow him the rest of his life. The man would sit in a populated area and beg for change while the townspeople would yell at him "you lazy nigger, you should feel ashamed!"

The man didn't lose his confidence or his desire to be free even though he was the only one in town living in poverty. One day the man sat in the same populated area he sat in before, but after this day he would not come back to sit there anymore. The man sat there as usual begging for a little change when all of a sudden a man appeared unto him, and after he saw him his life wouldn't be the same. The man that appeared had the world in his hand, and the man that appeared had for him a life-changing plan. The man that appeared could save his life, and the man that appeared was the Lord Jesus Christ. The man that sat begging stood up and wore his crown, and from that day forward no one could keep him down.

The End

The Well

There once was a woman who came to Jacob's well, her sin were greater than even she could tell. Many men had her, and many more wanted her too, but she had made up in her mind that she was through. Her lovers followed her to the well trying to get her to change her mind, but they didn't stand a chance fore she had already made up her mind. In their arms she was not truly happy, and she knew where true happiness would be, fore she had met a kind and giving man from Galilee. He made her no false promises and he told her no lies, and when she started crying he wiped every tear from her eyes. She had met her Messiah, she knew she had changed, but why did her life appear to her ex-lovers as being the same? Everywhere she would go and everything she would do she always had someone shouting out at her "hey, I remember you."

She would run back to the well feeling so much shame, and she would cry unto the Lord "I thought I've changed." The Lord would not respond, and she would walk away in grief, crying within herself "why won't the Lord answer me?" She would return to the well day after day crying and grieving over the same thing. Until one day the Lord decided to respond to her cry by appearing there by the well's side. She was crying with her head held down, she didn't even notice that he was around. "My child, why are you crying so? I've been standing here for a while and you didn't even know, and that's the same problem you're having accepting your new life. You are too concern about what others think about you to realize it was I who gave you eternal life."

The End

The Greatest Gift

There once was a young boy who felt so sad because he was not able to give great gifts to his dad. All his other siblings were able to give great expensive gifts, but all he could come up with was a wish I could get list. The dad was always pleased when he received those gifts, but his heart often grieved him because he knew that his younger son's heart was sick. The sickness of the young boy's heart became rottenness to his bones, and all he wanted to do was spend time alone. Sitting alone and idol resentment began to fill his heart, and the devotion he had with his dad began to fall apart. Their devotion fell apart so much there were times they didn't speak, and the young boy's heart began to hurt so much he didn't want to eat. This went on for several years until the young boy's father fell ill. Lying in a hospital bed his dad knew he needed to get real. Real about the broken relationship between him and his younger son, and real about the fact that his love cannot be bought or won. The dad called his younger son and begged to see his face, but the younger son refused saying "to you I've been nothing but a disgrace." The dad cried as he hung up the phone, and the dad died in his hospital bed all alone. The children gather around their dad's gravesite, and began to reminisce on his and their lives. Most of the children could only remember giving their dad great expensive gifts, but a real relationship with him they seemed to not be able to get. The younger son had time of remembering too, he knew all his dad had said and all his dad had done. Finally, it hit the young boy of how genuine his relationship was with his dad, "and that's the greatest gift they both ever had."

The End

You Can't Fly,
But We Can

There once was a girl who thought you had to have wings to fly, and without them you couldn't reach the sky. There was always a desire in her to soar above the rest, but without wings she felt less than her best. She would try out a new project, and just as she was about to reach her peck she would notice she had no wings, and began to sink. Her thoughts became discourage as she continued to try out new things because in her heart she placed the philosophy "she couldn't fly without wings." There was a man that notices her trying to soar above the ground, and he knew he could help her if she would come down. "Hey young lady, do you want to fly high?" Asked the man, but her being a few feet off the ground his words she didn't understand. "Come down!" The man said as he motioned with his hands. The girl came down, and listened to the man's plan. His plan was similar to her plan, but he added one extra thing instead of using the word "you" he added "we" to everything.

His plan worked perfectly as they soared across the evening sky and then the girl began to wonder "why by myself I couldn't soar this high?" The man reading her thoughts began to explain, "When you were trying to soar high alone it wasn't because you didn't have physical wings you failed, but it was because you didn't have spiritual wings you didn't excel." After the man finished talking he disappeared, and the girl was left alone in fear. A still small voice then spoke to her "fear not, fore it is God only that fails not."

The End

Persevere

There once was a man named Ed who couldn't get thoughts of defeat out of his head. He tried and tried to do so, but the past he couldn't let go. There were times in his life he felt he could succeed, but the fear in his heart caused him not to believe. Even though he had these fears he always would try, and even though he would fail he couldn't kiss his dreams good-bye. There always seemed to be a yearning deep within his heart and it was that yearning that wouldn't allow him to fall apart. Each morning he would wake up with his mind zeroed in on his dream even though he felt in that day he most likely wouldn't accomplish anything. He remained focus, and made a vow in his heart "I will not quit." He did everything in his power to prove that vow was legit. One day he took another step in the direction of his dream, and it was this step that would change everything.

The step he took seemed simple and it was something he never tried before, who'd ever thought it would be such a step that would even out the score. The step that he took he took in his heart, he began to say to himself "in order to have success failure must play apart," and it was in this declaration he finally felt free. And it was in overcoming his failures that proved how successful he really could be.

The End

The Pig that Wrapped Up His Own Blanket

There once was a racist cop it seemed like all most everyone knew, even most of the kids at his son's inner city school. A school in which his son like very well, and a school in which his son met two of his best black friends Shawn and Dell. The racist cop was unaware of his son having such friends; friends that his son vowed would be his friends to the very end. One day his son and his two black friends decided to prove others wrong by putting brown face paint on the cop's son and see if his father would do him any harm. They hung out where they knew his father would be, and they sat there for hours just shooting the breeze. When all of a sudden the racists cop rolled on the block, and came to a sudden stop. "What are you boys doing out here?" Asked the racist cop. Shawn and Dell's jaws suddenly locked. The racist cop's son feeling like it was all a joke rose up and said "nothing, just selling dope." The racist cop anode by the black kid's response got out of his car, and forced his son's face on the concrete block. His two black friends tried to tell the racist cop that it was his son, but the racist cop shouted at them "Shut up, if I wanted your opinion I would ask for one." The racist cop's son didn't know how to react, all he knew was he wanted his father's knee off his back, so he started to fight back. The racist cop thinking the black kid was going for his gun hit him twice in the head with his Billy club. After the second hit some of the face paint smeared off on to the club revealing half of the racist cop son's face. The racist cop's heart dropped as he beheld his son's half white, half black, bloody face, and then the racist cop cried in his heart "what have I done, how could I allow my hatred for others to cause me to hurt my own son!"

The End

Seeing is not Always Believing

There once was a woman named Red who didn't believe people could rise from the dead. She had no faith in supernatural things, and when people would try to tell her their experiences she would say something very mean. Her mind was closed to everything in which the world of science could not explain, and as for her thoughts on the religious community she thought they were all insane. She never tried to open her heart and listen to what Christian people had to say, and she didn't realize what they could have told her could have change her life one day. One day she decided to go to church with an old friend, when they arrived there service had just begun. The pastor was asking people to come up and testify and a woman about thirty years old walked up to the MIC. "Good morning church, my name is Sarah, and two days ago I was declared dead, but due to the goodness and greatness of God I now live!" Every believer in the church stood up and gave God praise, but Red in her heart question whether she was really dead in the first place. Red left a spirit fill morning service with a mind full of doubt. After she had got home she tried to sort things out. She looked in every scientific book she could find, but none was able to relieve her of the doubt in her mind. The next day she decided to go out to eat, she went to the same restaurant she ate at last week. While she sat there a man began to choke because of a big piece of meat stuck in his throat. The man died right there in the restaurant while his wife screamed his name, and the other people around them cried in pain. Suddenly a believer walked up and laid his hand on the dead man's shoulder and commanded him to live. The dead man open his eyes, the piece of meat fell out his mouth, and praises to God he began to give, but still Red was consumed with doubt questioning in her heart "would God go to the gates of death and bring someone out?"

The End

I'm More Than My Cover

There once was a boy who had a disability, and when some people looked at him that's all they wanted to see. He was a handsome, smart, and talented young man, but because of his disability he was despised, and tears never seemed to cease from falling from his eyes. He always wanted to be treated like everyone else, but the fear in others kept him confined to himself. One day he decided he was not going to let people ruin the person he was sent here to be, so he got up and went on a search for his destiny. While in search he discovered many great things about himself, and those discoveries helped him forget about the thoughts of everyone else. With his mind centered on his purpose he began to fulfill God's predestined plan, and he begun to reach heights no ones' mind could comprehend.

He was declared the best in everything he put his hands to, and there were no limits to what God through him was able to do. Many people could not understand how such greatness could come from a feeble, disabled young man, but in spite of their unbelief he continued to press on and succeed. He became the town's greatest wonder, they called him "wonder boy" to be exact because he rose up from his ashes and never looked back.

The End

His Heart, His Home

"Home is where the heart is." Mum, who ever said that must of knew there would be men like me. I am a man who didn't understand the true meaning of home until I lost it. If you haven't figured it out by now I'm homeless, and alone. I was not always this way, I had a good job making forty-five thousand a year, a beautiful wife, and four precious children. I guess you could say I was a real man back then, but now my only accomplishments are how many bottles of liquor I can drink in twenty-four hours. Looking back on my life I can see exactly where I went wrong, it was in my heart I lost the true meaning of home. I remember waking up in the morning seeing my beautiful wife's face, and caressing her soft but messy hair. She would open her eyes, and whisper in my ear "I love you" words that echo in my mind every-since the day I lost her. I also remember getting out of bed, and walking over to my children's rooms. There was nothing like watching their little faces light up when they saw me, and their love and adoration back then meant more than life to me. Now all I see in their eyes is shame when they see me, and that's more disappointing than my experiences. "Home is where the heart is," that is what someone said, but I feel selfish to even desire my home again. I'm sure my wife has moved on and my children the same; their hearts have been broken, and I am to blame. If I could have my heart back I would take it back in a heartbeat, but I can't because I saw my wife and children with another man last week. I guess his heart was in my home, and that is why I was led to leave it alone. I am where my heart desired to be, and I am where...............

The End

Stop Running From God!

There once was a child that decided at a very young age it didn't want to be saved. A foolish decision many around the child agreed, but still the child refused to let God fill its salvation need. The child grew older, and still the fool was attached to its back. There seemed to be no relief of the child's foolish acts. The child didn't want to clean up, go to school, nor have anything to do with the Lord and often it cuss out its parents whom it seemed to once adore. A few years later that child became an adult, and still the foolishness in its heart hadn't broken. An over groan fool is what the adult turned out to be because it wouldn't let God set it free. Many times God came to the adult showing his great mercy and love, but the adult wouldn't accept any messages from above. The adult grew older, and still had no desire to be saved.

Therefore, the adult became an old fool trying to find its way. The old fool being lost in the state of becoming physically blind became spiritually aware, fore she begun to see within herself God's presence there. Everything had to be taken from the old fool including her sight in order for her to see God's Guiding light. Seeing that light made her aware that truly there is a God out there, and if there is a God why wouldn't she want to be saved seeing it was him that put her on this earth for his purpose in the first place.

REPENT! AND BE SAVED.

Love,

Miatta Lynn Lansana

Notes

Notes

Notes

Notes

Notes

Notes